Silicon Armaged...

UNVEILING THE PERILS OF ARTIFICIAL INTELIGENCE, A THREAT BEYOND NUCLEAR WEAPON

Future Shockwave: AI's Threat Escalation Beyond the Nuclear Horizon

JAMES BRANDY

TABLE OF CONTENTS

INTRODUCTION

In the crucible of technological innovation, where the seeds of progress are sown, a formidable force has emerged, one that eclipses the existential fears of the past. Welcome to the age of "Silicon Armageddon: Unveiling the Perils of AI, a Threat Beyond Nuclear." As we stand on the precipice of a digital revolution, this book endeavors to unravel the intricate tapestry of artificial intelligence, exposing the profound risks it poses—risks that transcend the historic specter of nuclear annihilation.

The introductory chapters lay the foundation for our journey, charting the meteoric rise of artificial intelligence and the seismic shifts it has ushered into our collective consciousness. We explore the unprecedented power wielded by AI, a power that transcends mere computation, infiltrating the very fabric of our daily lives. From the evolution of machine learning to the intricacies of neural networks, we peel back the layers of innovation to reveal a double-edged sword—one capable of both unparalleled advancement and unprecedented peril.

In this paradigm-shifting exploration, we draw stark comparisons between the threats posed by artificial intelligence and those of the nuclear age. As we navigate through the chapters, we will delve into the potential ramifications of AI on a global scale, dissecting its economic, social, and political impacts. Yet, this journey is not one of mere alarmism; it is a call to awareness, a summons to confront the realities that lie ahead and take proactive measures to navigate the impending Silicon Storm.

Embark with us on this intellectual odyssey as we unmask the code-red threats of autonomous weapons, scrutinize algorithmic biases, and unravel the unforeseen consequences that loom in the shadow of artificial intelligence. Together, we shall explore the ethical quandaries that emerge and the regulatory challenges that demand our immediate attention. This is not a tale of doom but a narrative of empowerment, urging us to forge ethical frameworks, contemplate mindful innovation, and collectively shape a future where humanity triumphs in the face of Silicon Armageddon.

CHAPTER ONE

The Rise of Artificial Intelligence

In the annals of human history, certain epochs stand out as transformative, marked by the relentless pursuit of progress and innovation. The current era, defined by the rapid ascendance of artificial intelligence (AI), stands at the vanguard of such a revolution. This chapter serves as our portal into the heart of this digital renaissance, where the seeds of technological marvels blossom alongside the seeds of existential peril.

The narrative begins with a historical traverse, tracing the roots of AI from its inception to its present-day prominence. We unravel the threads of innovation woven by pioneers who dared to dream of machines that could emulate human intelligence. From Alan Turing's theoretical foundations to the advent of early computing, we witness the evolution of a concept that has now transcended the realm of science fiction, becoming an inextricable part of our reality.

As we delve deeper, we confront the awe-inspiring capabilities that AI now commands. Machine learning algorithms, fueled by vast datasets and computing power, exhibit an aptitude for tasks that were once exclusive to human cognition. The intricate dance of neural networks, modeled after the human brain, allows machines to decipher complex patterns, make decisions, and even engage in creative endeavors. This is the dawn of a new era, where the boundaries between artificial and human intelligence blur.

Yet, with the promise of progress comes an ominous shadow. The exponential growth of AI capabilities raises profound questions about the ethical implications and unforeseen consequences that accompany such power. This chapter compels us to confront the duality of AI—a force capable of groundbreaking advancements and, simultaneously, a harbinger of unprecedented threats.

As we stand at the crossroads of innovation and trepidation, the journey into the perils of Silicon Armageddon begins. The stage is set, and the actors are in position—AI's rise unfolds against the backdrop of a narrative that transcends the conventional fears of the nuclear age. Join us as we navigate through the intricate landscape of artificial intelligence, peeling back the layers to reveal a threat that surpasses the specter of nuclear annihilation, beckoning us into uncharted territory where the consequences of our digital creations are yet to be fully realized.

In the crucible of technological evolution, the genesis of AI danger emerges as a tale of unprecedented power, a narrative that unfolds with the allure of innovation but casts a shadow that stretches far beyond the boundaries of human foresight.

Section 1: Unprecedented Power: Understanding AI's Potential

The opening pages of our exploration delve into the unparalleled capabilities that artificial intelligence now commands. Here, we navigate through the intricate landscapes of machine learning and deep neural networks, deciphering the mechanisms that empower AI to exceed the limits of traditional computing. As algorithms evolve, driven by vast datasets and exponential increases in computing prowess, we witness a transformation—AI transcends mere computation to emulate human cognition. The once-distant realm of autonomous decision-making and problem-solving becomes the new frontier, promising efficiency and efficacy hitherto unimaginable.

However, with this unprecedented power comes a cascade of ethical dilemmas. W confront the capacity of AI to analyze, predict, and influence human behavior, raising profound questions about privacy, bias, and the very fabric of our societal structures. This section invites readers to grapple with the dual nature of AI—a tool of immense potential and a potential harbinger of unforeseen consequences.

Section 2: The Accelerating Pace: From Innovation to Menace

As the narrative unfolds, we pivot to the accelerating pace at which AI advances from a beacon of innovation to a looming menace. The relentless march of progress, fueled by a competitive drive for technological supremacy, propels us into uncharted territories. We witness the rapid deployment of AI across industries transforming economies, healthcare, education, and governance. This breakneck velocity, while promising untold benefits, raises critical concerns about the readiness of society to adapt to the transformative forces at play.

In this section, we explore the dichotomy between the positive potential and the looming peril. AI's ability to outpace human capabilities challenges our capacity to govern, regulate, and ethically harness its power. We scrutinize instances where innovation races ahead of ethical considerations, leaving a wake of unintended consequences that extend far beyond the initial intentions of its creators.

The third chapter sets the stage for our journey into the heart of Silicon Armageddon, where the uncharted waters of AI danger beckon. As we navigate through the nuanced landscape of unprecedented power and accelerating pace, the underlying question emerges: Can humanity stay ahead of the very creations it has birthed, or are we hurtling toward a future where the innovation that defines us becomes the menace that tests our resilience?

Section 1: Autonomous Weapons: The Armory of Tomorrow

In the echoing corridors of the digital age, the genesis of AI danger reaches a crescendo with the unveiling of autonomous weapons, the silent sentinels that blur the line between innovation and peril. As we dissect the fabric of this technological tapestry, we confront the profound implications of granting machines the autonomy to make life-altering decisions. From unmanned drones to AI-driven military strategies, we unravel the ethical conundrums and strategic risks that arise when the power to wage war is delegated to algorithms.

Section 2: Algorithmic Biases: Discrimination in the Digital Realm

The narrative deepens as we shift our focus to the insidious undercurrents within the AI landscape—algorithmic biases. Exploring the intricate interplay between data, algorithms, and societal structures, we unmask the subtle biases woven into the very code that shapes our digital reality. From discriminatory hiring practices to biased predictive policing, we confront the unsettling truth that AI, if not carefully curated, can perpetuate and exacerbate societal inequalities.

Section 3: Unintended Consequences: The Domino Effect of AI Actions

As we navigate through the labyrinth of AI's potential, we encounter the domino effect of unintended consequences. From healthcare algorithms inadvertently perpetuating medical disparities to AI-driven financial systems amplifying economic inequalities, we trace the ripples of unintended outcomes that reverberate through the fabric of our interconnected world. This section compels us to confront the unpredictability inherent in complex systems and the imperative to anticipate and mitigate the cascading impacts of AI actions.

CHAPTER FOUR

Redefining Ethics in the Age of Silicon Armageddon

Section 1: Ethical Frameworks: Navigating the Moral Abyss

As we continue our journey through the treacherous terrain of Code Red, the spotlight turns to the imperative of establishing robust Ethical Frameworks. In the wake of the revelations surrounding Autonomous Weapons, we grapple with the pressing need to navigate the moral abyss created by placing life-and-death decisions in the hands of machines. This section examines the ongoing efforts to define ethical guidelines that govern the development and deployment of AI, questioning whether humanity can construct a moral compass capable of guiding us through the perilous landscapes of the digital future.

Section 2: Regulatory Challenges: Navigating a Borderless Landscape

The exploration deepens as we confront the Regulatory Challenges inherent in taming the AI juggernaut. In the realm of Algorithmic Biases, where discrimination becomes embedded in the very code that shapes our digital reality, the call for regulatory frameworks intensifies. This section scrutinizes the complexities of establishing and enforcing regulations in a borderless landscape, where the rapid pace of innovation often outstrips the capacity of legal and regulatory mechanisms to keep pace.

Section 3: The Dual Nature of Regulation: Balancing Progress with Caution

As we unravel the Domino Effect of Unintended Consequences, we confront the dual nature of regulation—a delicate balancing act between fostering progress and exercising caution. This section probes the potential pitfalls of overregulation stifling innovation or under regulation leading to rampant risks. It explores the necessity of adaptive regulatory frameworks that evolve alongside AI advancements, ensuring the responsible development and deployment of technology without compromising the transformative potential it holds.

Chapter four encapsulates a critical juncture in our expedition through Code Red. It calls us to scrutinize the ethical foundations that underpin our technological pursuits and grapple with the intricate dance between regulatory measures and the dynamic nature of AI innovation. As we stand on the precipice of a future defined by the armory of autonomous weapons, the discriminatory biases within our digital fabric, and the cascading consequences of unintended actions, the challenge is clear: Can we forge ethical frameworks and regulatory landscapes robust enough to withstand the storms of Silicon Armageddon? The answers lie ahead, within the uncharted territories of an evolving ethical and regulatory frontier.

CHAPTER FIVE

Beyond Nuclear Nightmares

Section 1: A Comparative Analysis: AI vs. Nuclear Threats

In the crucible of existential anxieties, the chapter unfolds with a Comparative Analysis that transcends historical fears. We juxtapose the specter of artificial intelligence against the ominous shadows of nuclear threats. Drawing parallels and distinctions, this section seeks to unravel the unique nature of the dangers posed by AI, exploring how it diverges and converges with the perils that defined the nuclear age. As we traverse the landscapes of potential devastation, we illuminate the distinct challenges posed by the digital dawn.

Section 2: The Global Impact: Economic, Social, and Political Ramifications

The narrative deepens as we shift our focus to The Global Impact of AI, delving into the far-reaching ramifications across economic, social, and political realms. Unlike the localized threats of nuclear conflict, AI's influence spans borders, affecting every facet of our interconnected world. This section dissects the economic transformations brought about by AI automation, probes the social fabric reshaped by digital innovations, and scrutinizes the political landscapes shaped by the power dynamics of emerging technologies.

In this chapter, we confront the stark reality that the impact of Silicon Armageddon reaches far beyond the nightmares of nuclear warfare. The comparative analysis sheds light on the unprecedented challenges and opportunities ushered in by AI, forcing us to grapple with the complexities of a globalized, digitally-driven future. As we navigate through the intersections of AI and historical nuclear nightmares, the question emerges: Can humanity learn from the lessons of the past to chart a course toward a future where the perils of Silicon Armageddon are met with informed, global cooperation?

CHAPTER SIX

Navigating the Ethical and Regulatory Maze

Section 1: Ethical Frameworks: Can AI Be Tamed?

The journey into the heart of Silicon Armageddon intensifies as we confront the profound question that echoes through the corridors of technological innovation: Can AI Be Tamed? In this section, we delve into the labyrinth of Ethical Frameworks designed to navigate the moral terrain of artificial intelligence. As w witness the unprecedented power and potential pitfalls of AI, we scrutinize the ongoing efforts to establish ethical guidelines that ensure the responsible development, deployment, and use of this transformative technology. From the dilemmas of machine morality to the ethical implications of autonomous decision making, we unravel the complex tapestry of ethical considerations that seek to tame the untamed forces of artificial intelligence.

Section 2: Regulatory Challenges: Navigating a Borderless Landscape

The narrative takes a compelling turn as we confront the Regulatory Challenges that arise in the face of AI's unbridled potential. In a world where the digital landscape knows no borders, the task of creating and enforcing regulations becomes an intricate dance. This section explores the complexities of navigating a borderless landscape, where the pace of technological innovation often outstrips the ability of regulatory frameworks to keep pace. From data privacy concerns to the ethical use of AI in various industries, we dissect the regulatory maze that endeavors to strike a delicate balance between fostering progress and safeguardin against the perils of unfettered technological advancement.

Chapter six immerses us in the intricate interplay between ethical considerations and regulatory frameworks, painting a vivid portrait of the challenges faced in taming the formidable forces of artificial intelligence. As we grapple with the ethical implications and regulatory intricacies, the ultimate question persists: Can humanity, armed with ethical foresight and regulatory acumen, successfully navigate the borderless expanse of the digital landscape, or are we hurtling towards a future where the ethical and regulatory frameworks designed to tame AI become the last line of defense in the face of Silicon Armageddon?

Section 1: Ethical Frameworks: Can AI Be Tamed?

The journey into the heart of Silicon Armageddon intensifies as we confront the profound question that echoes through the corridors of technological innovation: Can AI Be Tamed? In this section, we delve into the labyrinth of Ethical Frameworks designed to navigate the moral terrain of artificial intelligence. As we witness the unprecedented power and potential pitfalls of AI, we scrutinize the ongoing efforts to establish ethical guidelines that ensure the responsible development, deployment, and use of this transformative technology. From the dilemmas of machine morality to the ethical implications of autonomous decision-making, we unravel the complex tapestry of ethical considerations that seek to tame the untamed forces of artificial intelligence.

Section 1: AI's Evolution: From Today to Tomorrow

The journey through Silicon Armageddon takes a forward-looking turn as we embark on a journey of Forecasting the Silicon Storm. In this section, we trace AI's Evolution, unraveling the threads of its past and present to discern the trajectory that lies ahead. From the infancy of machine learning to the sophisticated neural networks of today, we explore the pivotal moments that have defined AI's journey. With a keen eye on emerging trends and breakthroughs, we paint a portrait of the evolving landscape, offering insights into the technological forces that will shape the future of artificial intelligence. As we navigate through this temporal landscape, the question that looms large is: How will AI evolve from today to tomorrow, and what implications will this evolution have on the delicate balance between innovation and risk?

Section 2: Worst-Case Scenarios: Preparing for the Unthinkable

The narrative takes a sobering turn as we confront the shadows cast by the future—Worst-case scenarios that demand our attention and preparation. In this section, we explore the unthinkable possibilities, peering into a future where the perils of Silicon Armageddon reach their zenith. From scenarios of unchecked AI power to cataclysmic societal disruptions, we delve into the darkest corners of speculation. This is not a journey for the faint-hearted but a necessary exploration that compels us to consider the extreme possibilities, encouraging proactive measures to avert the direst outcomes. As we prepare for the unthinkable, we grapple with the ethical, societal, and existential challenges that may arise, equipping ourselves with the foresight needed to navigate the impending Silicon Storm.

Chapter Seven propels us into the realm of uncertainty and anticipation, where the future of artificial intelligence unfolds as a dynamic interplay between promise and peril. As we forecast the Silicon Storm, the chapter prompts reflection on our collective responsibility to guide AI's evolution and prepare for the unthinkable scenarios that may lie on the horizon. The journey into the future is both a cautionary tale and a call to action, urging us to navigate the uncharted territories of tomorrow with wisdom, foresight, and a steadfast commitment to the responsible stewardship of artificial intelligence.

CHAPTER EIGHT

Navigating the Future

Section 1: Collaborative Solutions: International Efforts in AI Governance

As we stand at the crossroads of technological evolution, Chapter Eight opens the gateway to Collaborative Solutions, recognizing the imperative of international cooperation in shaping the trajectory of AI governance. In this section, we explore the challenges and possibilities of forging alliances on a global scale. From policy harmonization to shared ethical frameworks, we delve into the collaborative initiatives that aim to create a unified front in addressing the challenges posed by artificial intelligence. As nations grapple with the complexities of regulating AI in an interconnected world, this section examines the potential for collaborative governance to ensure that the responsible use of AI becomes a shared global commitment.

Section 2: Hope in the Digital Age: Shaping a Responsible AI Future

The narrative takes an optimistic turn as we delve into the possibilities that lie within the Digital Age. "Hope in the Digital Age" explores the transformative potential of technology to uplift humanity. From innovative applications in healthcare and education to the promise of AI-driven solutions addressing pressing global challenges, this section showcases how responsible and ethically guided development of AI can be a beacon of hope. By examining case studies and initiatives that prioritize positive impact, we navigate a future where AI becomes a force for good, contributing to the betterment of society, environmental sustainability, and the well-being of individuals.

Chapter eight serves as a compass for Navigating the Future, emphasizing the need for international collaboration in the governance of AI and inspiring hope in an era defined by digital innovation. The collaborative solutions we forge today and the responsible deployment of AI offer a glimpse into a future where technology aligns with human values, contributing to a world that thrives on the principles of ethical innovation and shared responsibility. As we navigate the uncharted waters of the future, this chapter invites us to envision a path where the transformative power of AI becomes a force that fosters global well-being and collective progress.

CHAPTER NINE

Reflections and Responsibilities

In the penultimate chapter of "Silicon Armageddon: Unveiling the Perils of AI, a Threat Beyond Nuclear," we transition from the shadows of fear to the illumination of ethical innovation. This chapter serves as a beacon, guiding us through the necessary transformation from apprehension to proactive, responsible action in the face of the challenges posed by artificial intelligence.

Section 1: The Ethical Imperative

As we embark on this chapter, we delve into The Ethical Imperative. Here, we explore the foundational principles that underpin responsible innovation in the realm of AI. From ensuring transparency and accountability to prioritizing human-centric values, this section emphasizes the ethical imperatives that must guide the development, deployment, and governance of artificial intelligence. By examining real-world cases where ethical considerations have steered positive outcomes, we illuminate a path forward that embraces technology while safeguarding human dignity.

Section 2: Fostering a Culture of Responsibility

The narrative deepens as we examine the critical role of fostering a Culture of Responsibility. From individual developers to multinational corporations, this section underscores the importance of cultivating a collective consciousness that prioritizes the ethical implications of AI technologies. By encouraging transparency, accountability, and a commitment to societal well-being, we lay the groundwork for a culture where innovation aligns with responsible practices, mitigating the risks associated with Silicon Armageddon.

Section 3: From Crisis to Opportunity

The chapter crescendos with a transformational perspective, transitioning "Silicon Armageddon" from a crisis narrative to a realm of opportunity. By recognizing the potential for positive change, innovation becomes a catalyst for societal betterment. From addressing global challenges to fostering inclusivity and diversity in technological development, this section illuminates the vast opportunities that lie within the ethical and responsible deployment of AI. As we redefine the narrative, the question arises: Can we shift the trajectory of Silicon Armageddon from a foreboding threat to a future defined by the transformative and positive potential of artificial intelligence?

Chapter nine serves as a call to action—a summons to embrace ethical innovation, cultivate a culture of responsibility, and recognize the opportunities that arise from responsible AI deployment. As we navigate the delicate balance between fear and optimism, this chapter beckons us to contribute to a future where the perils of Silicon Armageddon are met with the ethical fortitude needed to ensure a harmonious coexistence between humanity and artificial intelligence.

CHAPTER TEN

Towards a Harmonious Future

As we reach the culmination of "Silicon Armageddon: Unveiling the Perils of AI, a Threat Beyond Nuclear," Chapter Twelve beckons us toward the vision of a Harmonious Future. In this concluding chapter, we explore the pathways to reconciliation between humanity and the transformative force of artificial intelligence, aiming for a future where innovation aligns seamlessly with ethical considerations.

Section 1: Bridging the Gap: Human-AI Collaboration

The journey towards a harmonious future begins with Bridging the Gap, emphasizing the potential of Human-AI Collaboration. By recognizing AI as a tool to augment human capabilities rather than replace them, we explore the collaborative possibilities that arise when humans and machines work in tandem. From healthcare advancements to creative partnerships, this section showcases the symbiotic relationship that can emerge, fostering a future where AI complements human ingenuity rather than competing with it.

Section 2: Empowering Society: Inclusive and Ethical AI

The narrative deepens as we focus on Empowering Society through Inclusive and Ethical AI. This section advocates for the development and deployment of AI technologies that prioritize inclusivity, diversity, and ethical considerations. By addressing algorithmic biases, ensuring fair representation, and involving diverse perspectives in AI development, we lay the foundation for a future where technology becomes a force for societal empowerment and upliftment.

Section 3: Sustaining Innovation: Ethical Governance and Adaptability

The chapter crescendos with an exploration of Sustaining Innovation through Ethical Governance and Adaptability. Here, we delve into the necessity of robust ethical governance frameworks that evolve alongside AI innovations. By fostering adaptability, accountability, and continuous ethical scrutiny, we navigate toward a future where the transformative power of AI sustains innovation without compromising ethical principles. This section challenges us to rethink governance structures, encouraging a dynamic and responsive approach to the ever-evolving landscape of artificial intelligence.

In this chapter, the narrative shifts from unveiling perils to embracing the potential for a harmonious coexistence with AI. As we envision a future where innovation is guided by ethical considerations, collaboration between humans and machines thrives, and society is empowered and uplifted, the journey through "Silicon Armageddon" concludes on a note of optimism and responsibility. The question that lingers is whether humanity can collectively navigate toward this harmonious future, where the promise of AI is harnessed for the greater good of all.

CHAAPTER ELEVEN

A Collective Covenant

In the final chapter of "Silicon Armageddon: Unveiling the Perils of AI, a Threat Beyond Nuclear," we delve into the concept of A Collective Covenant, a pact forged by humanity to navigate the challenges and potentials of artificial intelligence with wisdom, responsibility, and a shared commitment to a harmonious future.

Section 1: The Covenant of Ethical Stewardship

The journey begins with The Covenant of Ethical Stewardship, emphasizing the collective responsibility to act as ethical stewards of AI. As custodians of innovation, individuals, organizations, and governments are urged to uphold the principles of transparency, accountability, and inclusivity. This section explores the establishment of ethical frameworks and governance structures that transcend borders, fostering a global commitment to ensuring that AI serves humanity's best interests.

Section 2: Nurturing Technological Literacy and Informed Citizenship

A critical component of the collective covenant is Nurturing Technological Literacy and Informed Citizenship. In this section, we explore the imperative of equipping individuals with the knowledge and understanding required to navigate the complexities of the digital age. By promoting informed citizenship, societies can actively participate in shaping the ethical landscape of AI, fostering a culture where individuals contribute to the responsible development and deployment of technology.

Section 3: Global Collaboration: A United Front Against Perils

The narrative crescendos with a call for Global Collaboration—a United Front Against Perils. Recognizing the borderless nature of AI challenges, this section advocates for increased collaboration between nations, industries, and researchers. By sharing knowledge, resources, and best practices, the international community can collectively address the potential perils of Silicon Armageddon, fostering a sense of unity in safeguarding the future of humanity.

Epilogue: The Ongoing Saga of Ethical Innovation

The book concludes with an Epilogue that recognizes the ongoing saga of Ethical Innovation. As the digital landscape evolves, so too must our ethical considerations and governance structures. This final section underscores the dynamic nature of the collective covenant, urging continued vigilance, adaptability, and a steadfast commitment to ethical innovation as we navigate the unfolding chapters of Silicon Armageddon.

"Silicon Armageddon: Unveiling the Perils of AI, a Threat Beyond Nuclear" concludes not as a prophecy of doom but as a call to action. The collective covenant emerges as a blueprint for a future where humanity and artificial intelligence coexist harmoniously, guided by ethical principles, informed citizenship, and a commitment to fostering a world where innovation serves the greater good.

Conclusion: Safeguarding Humanity in the Age of Silicon Armageddon

In concluding our journey through the intricate landscapes of artificial intelligence in "Recapitulation: The Dual Nature of AI," we find ourselves at a crossroads, standing on the precipice of an unprecedented era—the Age of Silicon Armageddon. This exploration has uncovered the dual nature of AI, revealing its immense potential for positive transformation alongside the inherent perils that cast shadows on our collective future.

As we recapitulate the intricate nuances explored throughout this journey, we confront the reality that artificial intelligence is not merely a tool but a profound force that mirrors the complexity of humanity itself. From the transformative power that can revolutionize industries, healthcare, and education to the ethical dilemmas that echo through algorithms shaping our societal structures, the dual nature of AI reflects both the promise and peril encapsulated within our pursuit of technological advancement.

The call to action resounds as a clarion summons—a collective responsibility to Safeguard Humanity. In the face of Silicon Armageddon, this call extends beyond governments and industries to every individual inhabiting this interconnected world. As stewards of innovation, we must recognize the ethical imperative to ensure that the trajectory of artificial intelligence aligns with human values, dignity, and flourishing.

A Blueprint for Ethical Innovation:

Fostering Transparency and Accountability: Embrace a culture of transparency in the development and deployment of AI, holding creators accountable for the consequences of their innovations.

Prioritizing Ethical Governance: Advocate for the establishment and continuous refinement of ethical governance frameworks that adapt to the evolving nature of AI, ensuring responsible use and safeguarding against unintended consequences.

Nurturing Technological Literacy: Promote widespread technological literacy to empower individuals with the knowledge needed to make informed decisions, fostering a society that actively participates in shaping the ethical landscape of AI.

Global Collaboration: Recognize the borderless nature of AI challenges and actively engage in global collaboration. By sharing insights, resources, and ethical best practices, humanity can stand united against the perils of Silicon Armageddon.

Inclusive and Diverse Innovation: Champion inclusive and diverse innovation, ensuring that the development of AI technologies reflects the richness of human experiences and minimizes biases that may perpetuate societal inequalities.

As we navigate the uncharted waters of the Age of Silicon Armageddon, this conclusion is not the end but a commencement—a commencement of a collective endeavor to shape a future where the dual nature of AI becomes a harmonious force for human progress. In the hands of ethical stewards, artificial intelligence has the potential to elevate humanity to unprecedented heights. The question that lingers is whether we, as custodians of innovation, are ready to shoulder the responsibility and safeguard humanity in the age defined by the transformative potential of Silicon Armageddon.